The Young Naturalist
Neil Arnold

Ward Lock Limited · London

Text © Neil Arnold 1983
Illustrations © Ward Lock Limited 1983

First published in Great Britain in 1983
by Ward Lock Limited, 82 Gower Street,
London WC1E 6EQ, a Pentos Company.

All Rights Reserved. No part of this publication
may be reproduced, stored in a retrieval system,
or transmitted, in any form or by any means,
electronic, mechanical, photocopying, recording,
or otherwise, without the prior permission of the
Copyright owners.

Layout by Jude Fletcher
House editor Suzanne Kendall
The illustrations were prepared by Chris Shields
and Roger H. Coggins of Wilcock Riley.
Text filmset in Century Schoolbook
by M & R Computerised Typesetting Ltd, Grimsby
Printed and bound in Italy
by Sagdos SpA

British Library Cataloguing in Publication Data
Arnold/Neil
   The young naturalist.
   1. Natural history
   I. Title
   508   QH48
   ISBN 0-7063-6219-5

Contents

Watching animals   4

Insects, birds and mammals   6

Butterflies and moths   8
   The life cycle   10
   Feeding   12
   Finding butterflies and moths   14
   Catching insects   16

How to watch birds   18
   Identifying birds   20
   Counting birds   22
   Migration   24
   Feeding birds   26
   Birds breeding   28
   Birds in flight   30
   Birds' beaks   32
   Birds' feet   34

Mammals in the garden   36
   Small mammals   38
   Collecting evidence   40
   Watching mammals   42

Animals living together – an Oak tree   44

Animals living together – a downland   46

Suggested further reading and useful addresses   48

Watching animals

There is a good chance that you live in a town and if you do you probably think there is no wildlife near home for you to watch. But town parks, gardens, factory sites, canal banks and railway edges are full of life. However, before you set off be sure that you are going to be safe. Watch factory sites and railways from *outside* the fence and keep well away from the edge of canals. If you are going to a park, go with a friend. Remember to tell your family where you are going.

Many plants which grow in odd corners, such as Rosebay Willowherb, are very attractive to insects. Look out for Buddleia growing from walls or on waste ground – the purple flowers are sure to be covered with butterflies on a bright, sunny day.

There is a good variety of birds in towns. Ducks, Coot and Moorhen on park lakes, Thrushes and Warblers in shrubberies and Wagtails, House Sparrows, Starlings and Blackbirds in the streets. House Sparrows are often found searching for seeds on the pavements and flower beds.

The Blackbird patrols lawns, leaning its head to one side, listening for the tell-tale movements of worms, or searching for slugs and berries. The Pied Wagtail is always on the move, catching ground-feeding insects. Overhead, House Martins trawl for flying insects and Starlings fly in from the countryside to roost on tall buildings in the city centre. Don't forget Pigeons – they are always present in towns and make a good subject for study.

In the countryside, where people and buildings are fewer, wildlife abounds. Dragonflies develop in ponds until they change their coats for the last time, revealing delicate wings and colourful bodies. Look for plants with holes in their leaves and you are sure to find caterpillars. Turn over fallen logs and wet leaves and see the centipedes and woodlice run from the light. But remember to replace the log and leaves before you go.

Up in the trees the Treecreeper examines strips of bark and the Great-spotted Woodpecker drills holes in search of grubs. The Redstart and Willow Warbler, summer visitors to Britain and Europe, eat insects among the leaves and twigs. The Jay, ever alert, searches for acorns, which it buries in its winter store. High overhead the Kestrel hovers, watching the ground for the movement of mice and voles. A squirrel gathers nuts and a fox stalks across the pasture. As night falls the Tawny Owl stirs from its perch. Flapping with silent wings it flies through the wood calling 'Ke-wick' to keep in contact with other owls and in the hope that startled mice and voles will give away their positions.

Insects, birds and mammals

The whole animal kingdom can be divided into two groups. Those without backbones, such as insects, are called invertebrates, and those with backbones, such as birds and mammals, are called vertebrates. Invertebrates have soft bodies which are often protected by hard shells or by a horny outer skeleton. Vertebrates have soft bodies which are supported by an internal column.

Insects are in a group of invertebrates known as arthropods, which means 'jointed feet', but not only are the legs jointed, so is the whole body. An insect's body is divided into three main sections, the head, the thorax and the abdomen. The head carries a pair of sensitive antennae which help the insect to smell, touch (or feel) and know its position when flying. It also carries some sort of biting or sucking mouth and a pair of eyes. The chest-like thorax carries three pairs of walking legs and sometimes wings. The abdomen contains the stomach of the insect.

Insects give birth to young by laying eggs. Generally these hatch into larvae which then change into adults (see page 11). This is not always the case, however, as some species allow the eggs to develop in their bodies and 'give birth' to live young, which look like the adults. There are over a million species of insects in the world and because of this they are an important source of food for other animals.

All animals heat their bodies by 'burning' food. Some, though, are cold-blooded and they need the heat of the sun to warm them and make them active. Insects are cold-blooded and therefore are at their most active during the summer months.

Birds are animals with feathers. The large feathers in the wing are strong and flexible, enabling the bird to fly, while the fluffy body

Water Plantain

Mayfly

Emperor Dragonfly

A juvenile Golden Eagle

feathers help to preserve their body heat. The wings of birds are 'arms' with which they fly, swim, or use as balancers as in the case of the flightless running birds such as the Ostrich. Wings are powered by heavy chest muscles. Birds have light feathers and hollow bones so that they are light enough to fly. They need to eat great quantities of food to obtain the energy to power their flight. Their eggs are covered in a waterproof shell and contain a rich food. They are laid, to develop outside the female's body. Breeding birds in the cool temperatures of Europe sit on their eggs to keep them warm. In warmer countries they may also sit on the eggs but in this case it is to shade them from the sun.

Mammals are animals with hair. They have a layer of fat beneath the skin and hair surrounding the body to keep heat in. Mammals give birth to young which have developed within the female's body. At birth, mammals look like their parents and are sometimes able to look after themselves. While very young, though, the mother feeds them with milk from her body – this is true of all mammals whether they swim, fly or live on the land. The human is a mammal who at birth is in need of a great deal of care which must continue through a long childhood.

Look at the pictures. Dragonflies and Mayflies develop in water from eggs laid on water plants. The nymphs (larvae) of Mayflies feed on water weeds and microscopic plants. When they are mature they float on the water surface, their skin splits and the winged adult crawls out. The adults do not feed and often only live a day or two, just long enough to mate and lay their eggs. Dragonfly nymphs are ferocious hunters, living on invertebrates and small fish. When mature they climb from the water on to a plant stem, their skin splits and the winged adult appears. The adult hunts other insects in flight.

The Golden Eagle is a bird of prey which soars high over mountain areas on the lookout for hares and grouse. When the bird has spotted its prey it glides down and carries it away with its sharp talons.

Badgers (like most humans) are omnivores and will eat almost anything they can find. Their diet includes small mammals, roots, fruit, insects and birds' eggs.

Omnivores—badgers eating fruit and a small mammal

Butterflies and moths

Butterflies and moths are probably the easiest insects to get to know at first hand – as they are very common and often eye-catching. They make up the family Lepidoptera. The members of this family are insects having two pairs of scaly wings and a long, coiled, sucking mouth called a proboscis. They also have 'hairy' bodies and a prominent head containing large compound eyes – that is eyes made up of a collection of smaller eyes. They also have very obvious antennae or 'feelers'. All butterflies and moths are able to fly except for the females of a few moth species. These females have very small wings and can only crawl about on the trees and woodland floors on which they live.

Butterflies and moths appear to be very similar. But they can be told apart if carefully studied. Butterflies have knobs on the end of their antennae. Moths have antennae of many shapes but they *never* have knobs on the end. There is also another great difference. The wings of butterflies move freely as they are not joined to one another. The wings of moths, however, are joined with a bristle or a group of bristles so that they operate together. You will only be able to see this if you examine a dead moth or one you have caught.

Butterflies and moths often die when trapped in rooms or buildings. These will give you a few specimens to study during the winter months. If you want to catch butterflies or moths you must use a net, as catching them with your hands or a hat is sure to injure them. When you have examined the butterfly or moth release it outside in the place in which it was caught. This is very important as breeding butterflies defend a territory – an area which is 'theirs' and from which they chase off all other butterflies of the same species. If you just release them at random they may find it difficult to regain their territory.

Another difference between butterflies and moths is the way in which they hold their wings when resting. Butterflies fold their wings vertically (upright) over their backs so

The antennae of butterflies and moths

Cinnabar moth
Marbled White butterfly
Large Skipper butterfly

that the colourful upper surfaces touch. This leaves only the dull lower surface of the wings showing, helping the insect to escape detection. This is particularly noticeable in the Peacock butterfly. Moths fold their wings horizontally (flat) so that the lower wings lie over the insect's body and the upper wings cover them – the Scalloped Oak is typical. Some moths, however, are able to fold their wings around their bodies, giving the insect a barrel shape. The Buff Tip moth is one of these – when sitting on the end of a branch it looks just like a broken twig. Some species, such as the Chinese Character moth, look just like a bird dropping and are therefore unattractive to birds! Many of the smaller moths resemble insects of totally different families, such as caddis flies, hornets and bees. This skill at camouflage confuses their usual enemies who would eat them if only they knew!

Sometimes it is hard to tell which is which because a number of moths resemble butterflies and some butterflies look like moths. The Skipper butterflies often hold their wings flat over their bodies or just slightly raised; this gives them a moth-like appearance. Some moths, especially those of the thorn family, hold their wings together vertically over their backs and look remarkably like butterflies. If you are in doubt look at all the other features of the insect before deciding whether you should look it up in the butterfly or moth section of your field guide book.

Don't assume that all the lepidoptera you see in the daytime are butterflies. Many moths fly regularly in the day and many night-flying species will fly in the daytime if disturbed from their hiding place. The Cinnabar moth is a day-flying species. When sunning themselves, to become warm enough for flight, butterflies hold their four wings out horizontally from the body, showing off their fine colours, while moths usually reveal only their upper wings.

The life cycle

Male butterflies attract a mate with the bright colours on the upper surface of the wings. Even those species like the 'whites' and 'browns', which appear dull have areas of contrasting colour which can be flashed in the sunlight. Female moths produce a strong scent which is wafted through the air until detected by the large antennae of the male. Some moths have been known to fly more than a kilometre in order to find the female giving off the scent. When the pair meet they join their abdomens to mate. They remain in this position while flying and the egg is fertilized by the male sperm.

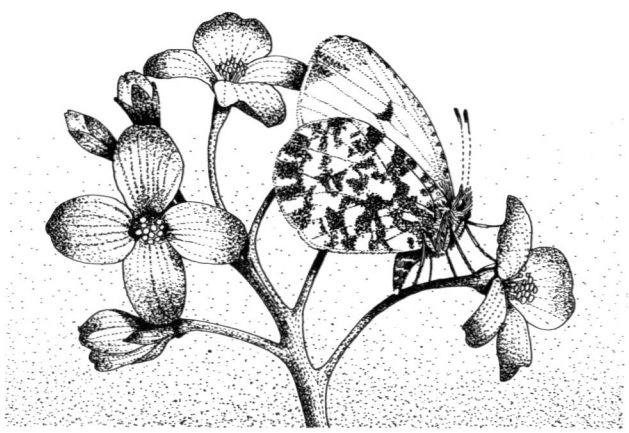

An Orange Tip butterfly laying an egg on Lady's Smock

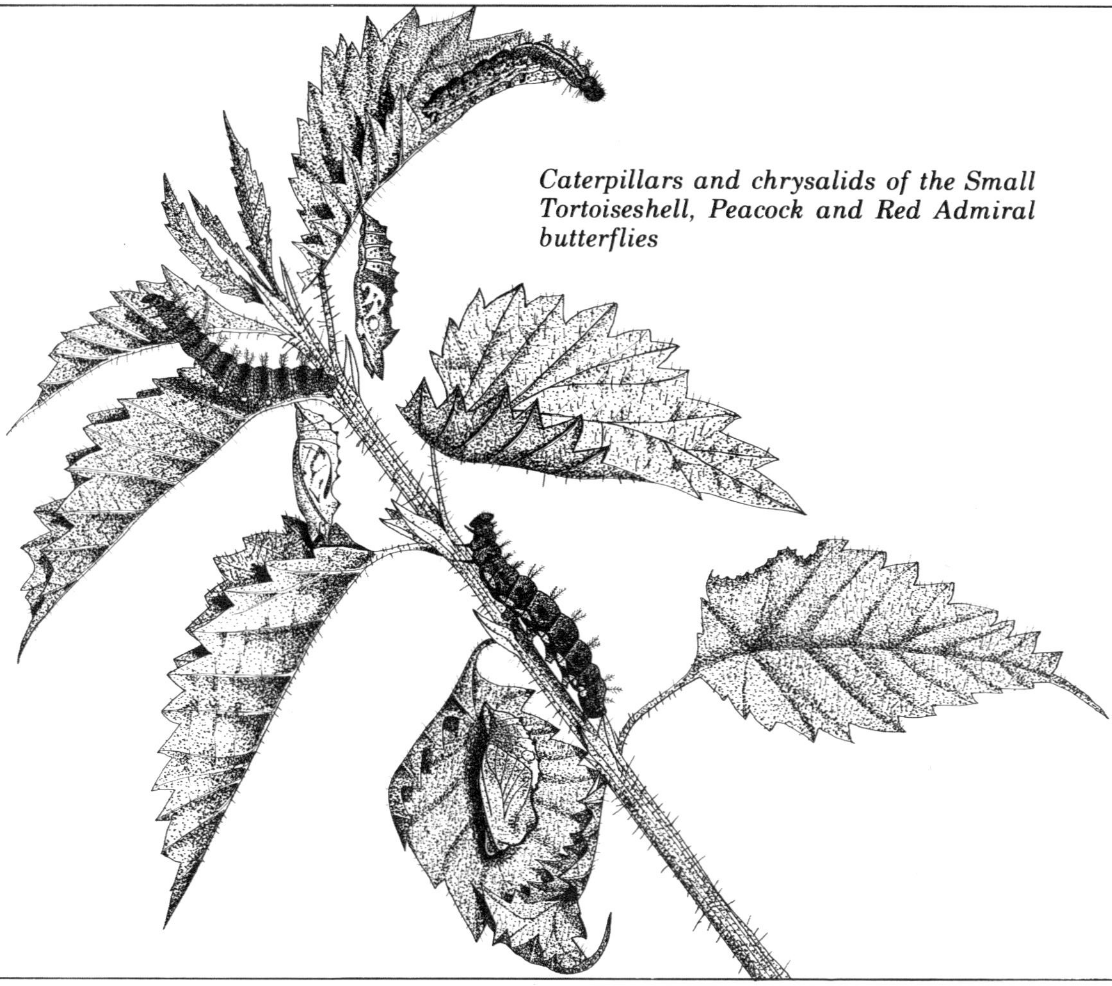

Caterpillars and chrysalids of the Small Tortoiseshell, Peacock and Red Admiral butterflies

The life history of the Small Tortoiseshell butterfly

The females are able to 'taste' plants through their feet and will lay their eggs on suitable plants. In some cases it may be a group of plant species, say the grasses, in other cases only one species like the Stinging Nettle. Some insects lay their eggs singly, some in clusters. The Orange Tip lays a single egg on each stem of Lady's Smock, while the Small Tortoiseshell lays a cluster of green eggs on a leaf of the nettle.

Insects, unlike birds and mammals, are not born with the same shape that they will have as fully-grown adults. They develop in a number of stages through a process called metamorphosis during which their bodies undergo great changes. Below is what happens in the life cycle of a butterfly or moth.

After a while (a time which can vary between a few days or a few months) the eggs hatch and the minute caterpillars (the larvae) emerge and immediately begin to feed on the egg shell and then on the host plant. After some days of growth the caterpillar builds a shell around its body and becomes a chrysalis or pupa. The body of the caterpillar breaks down within this pupa and is reformed into the adult insect. When this process is finished the adult butterfly splits open the skin of the chrysalis and emerges. It then pumps blood through the veins of its wings, inflating them. It allows them to dry and harden, and then flies off to mate and start the cycle all over again.

Green-veined White butterflies mating

11

Feeding

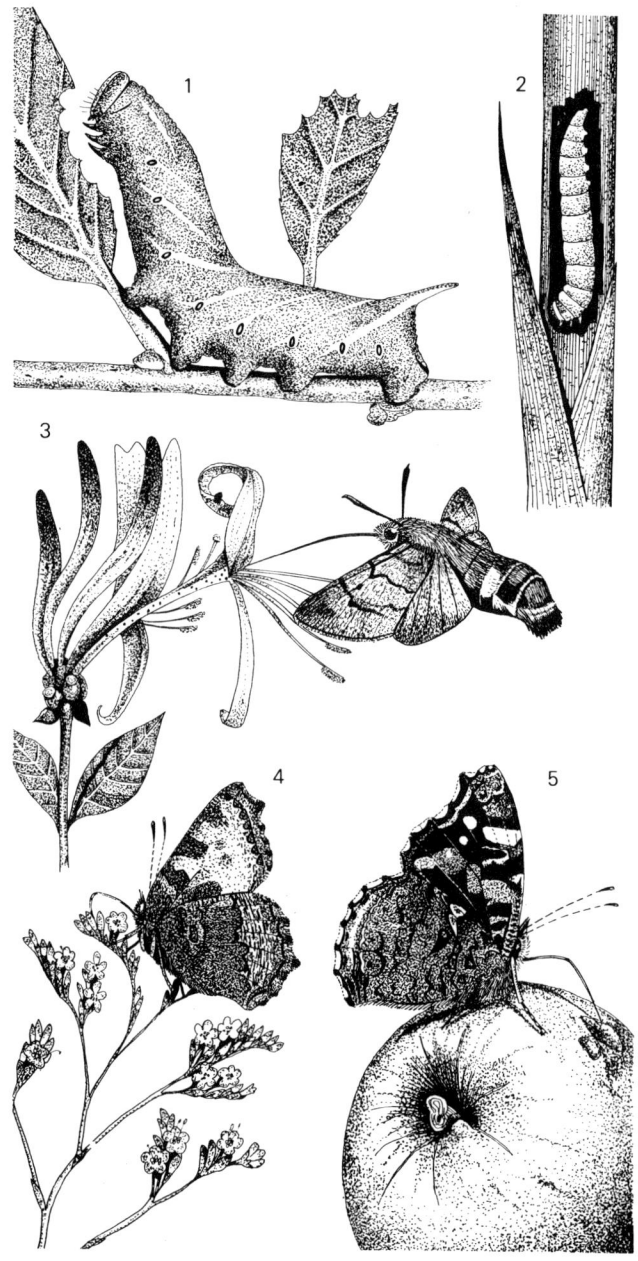

Butterflies and moths feed mainly on plants so it is essential to learn the names of some common wild plants. The best way to do this is to sit and watch the insects in every stage of their development and then try and identify the plants they visit. If you cannot find the picture in a plant book get an adult to help you. Always take the book to the plant rather than picking the plant and taking it home to identify.

The plants caterpillars feed on are known as 'larval food plants' – the plants the larvae feed on. Once you get to know some of these plants studying insect feeding will become much easier. Perhaps the easiest plant to start with is the Stinging Nettle. It is the home of the caterpillars of the colourful Peacock butterfly, Small Tortoiseshell, Red Admiral and Comma. You will also know the cabbage which attracts members of the 'white' family of butterflies.

Once the caterpillars have eaten the egg case they find themselves on their food plant. They then use their biting jaws to eat their way through the leaves. Look on shrubs and you will sometimes find a series of leaf skeletons, the caterpillars having eaten everything but the leaf veins. The caterpillar of the Bulrush Wainscot moth even feeds within the stem of its food plant. As caterpillars grow they shed their skins and then fill out their new softer covering. Once they have reached maturity (as a caterpillar) they enter the non-feeding period of their lives in the pupa.

The adult insect which emerges has no chewing mouth parts but a long tubular tongue called a proboscis. When not in use this 'tongue' is rolled into a coil, much like an out-of-use hosepipe. When it is ready to feed it unrolls its tongue and probes the base of a flower for the sweet juice called nectar. Butterflies and moths feed on simple flowers like those of Bramble and Honeysuckle, being unable to penetrate the complex flowers of

1 An Eyed Hawk moth caterpillar feeding on Sallow
2 A Bulrush Wainscot moth caterpillar inside the rush
3 A Humming-bird Hawk moth feeding on Honeysuckle nectar
4 A Small Tortoiseshell butterfly feeding on Lavender nectar
5 A Red Admiral butterfly feeding on the juices of a rotten apple

many garden plants. Some butterfly species will feed on the energy-rich juices of rotting fruit, animal droppings and even on human sweat.

At first you will find it difficult to watch the feeding process as the proboscis is very thin and difficult to pick out. For a while you may find it useful to list the plants which are visited by a particular insect species and then later try to watch feeding in progress. It is also important to notice how the adult insect moves on from one food plant to another as the season progresses and different plants come into flower.

See if you can discover whether butterflies prefer white flowers to red, yellow or blue. Many plants have lines along the petals leading to the base of the flower and the nectar. These are known as 'guide lines' and are designed to lead insects to the plant's food. Mother Nature has not designed flowers entirely for the benefit of insects though, for as the insects feed they carry the pollen of one flower to the next so aiding the production of fertile seeds.

If you really want to study insect feeding try growing a selection of food plants in your garden. Even a few carefully selected flowers in a tub or window box will attract insects. The most attractive garden plants include purple Aubrietia, yellow Alyssum, Arabis, Wallflowers, Primroses, Sweet Rocket, Valerian, Honesty, Petunias, the Ice Plant and purple Buddleia. If you only have room for one shrub choose Buddleia. Small patches of Thistle and Bramble in the garden are also bound to attract insects.

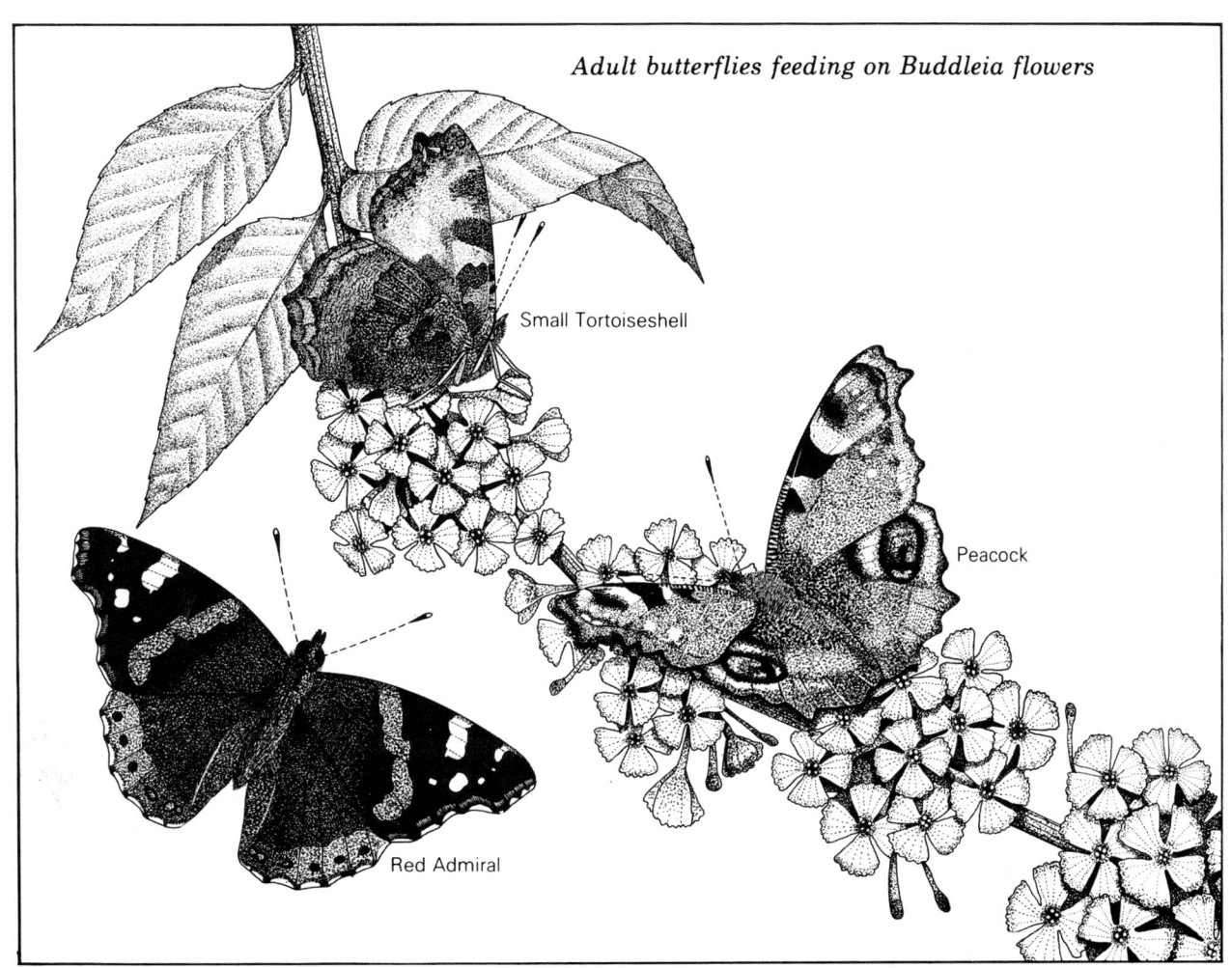

Adult butterflies feeding on Buddleia flowers

Finding butterflies and moths

Finding insects requires the skills of the hunter, a knowledge of the place, careful movement, patient watching and, most of all, some idea of what you are looking for. To start with you will only see the obvious but as you improve your techniques you will begin to discover those insects which are making an effort to remain unseen.

Hunting for butterflies would appear simple but that is not necessarily so, many species are not willing to show off their colours and others live high among the tree-tops, seldom coming down to ground level.

When feeding or sunning themselves butterflies position themselves in line with the warming rays of the sun. It is then that they show off their fine colours in an effort to attract a mate. It is also at this moment that they are at most risk from birds, reptiles and small mammals. As a defence against harmful attack butterflies have bright bars of colour or colourful 'eyes' at the tips of their wings – this is to encourage attackers to strike at the wings instead of aiming at their soft, fragile bodies. You will find many butterflies which seem fit and healthy despite their tattered wings, shredded by attacking birds.

Butterflies are very colourful in flight but, as soon as they settle they 'disappear'. As they fold their wings only the camouflaged undersides of the wings are visible. This is especially true of the Heathland Greyling which, once settled, not only displays its mottled underwings but adjusts its position to the sun so that it casts no shadow. The Orange Tip butterfly has green and white mottled underwings which instantly merge with the sun-speckled background. Species such as the Brimstone and Comma settle on plants, resembling fresh yellow or dead brown leaves. Even the outline of their wings helps them deceive those animals that hunt them.

Most moths hide in the daytime so their upper wings resemble the background against which they hope to conceal themselves. The Angleshades has patterned wings which enable it to disappear into a background of leaf litter on the woodland floor. The Garden Tiger moth on the other hand has bright contrasting colours which make it stand out. This moth is nasty tasting and its colours warn attackers that it is not good to eat.

It is often possible to see butterflies and

Brimstone butterfly

Comma butterfly

Garden Tiger moth

Greyling butterfly

Angleshades moth

day-flying moths just by sitting down quietly and waiting for them to come to you. Most of these insects are territorial, patrolling a small, fixed area. Watching one of these areas will enable you to study the details of butterfly behaviour.

Once you get to know the adult insects and their larval food plants you will soon find the eggs, caterpillars and pupa. Some caterpillars will be difficult to find as they are very well camouflaged. Try to find the caterpillars of the 'white' family on cabbage leaves to start with. The caterpillars of the Small Tortoiseshell butterfly are also easy to find because they live in a silk web on the leaves of the Stinging Nettle. The caterpillars of the Cinnabar moth are especially obvious as they have orange and black markings which indicate their foul taste.

Caterpillars can also be gathered by beating a branch with a stick and catching the falling insects on a white sheet. Don't forget to look out for the Looper moth caterpillars which hang from trees by a thread. Some pupae which live in the soil can only be found by digging at the base of suitable trees, others will be attached to vegetation. It is very important that you read about the habits of the species that you are trying to find.

Looking for eggs

TOP *Orange Tip butterfly eggs on Lady's Smock*
CENTRE *Small Tortoiseshell butterfly eggs on nettle*
ABOVE *Buff Ermine eggs on dock*

Searching for larvae

Catching insects

'Sugaring'

Many adult insects (which in books are sometimes called imago) are difficult to identify both in flight and at rest. The task is made easier though if they are captured. Remember, though, that when catching insects their welfare is the first consideration.

Butterflies can be caught in nets. They can either be captured as they rest on plants or whilst in flight. When catching the butterfly in flight the net is swept across the path of the insect's flight and then turned at right angles to close the mouth of the net. When catching a butterfly at rest the mouth of the net should be lowered over the insect while the other hand holds the point of the net up in the air so that the captive will fly up into the body of the net. Take care not to catch butterflies on Bramble bushes or your net will be torn to shreds!

'Lamping'

Netting butterflies and moths

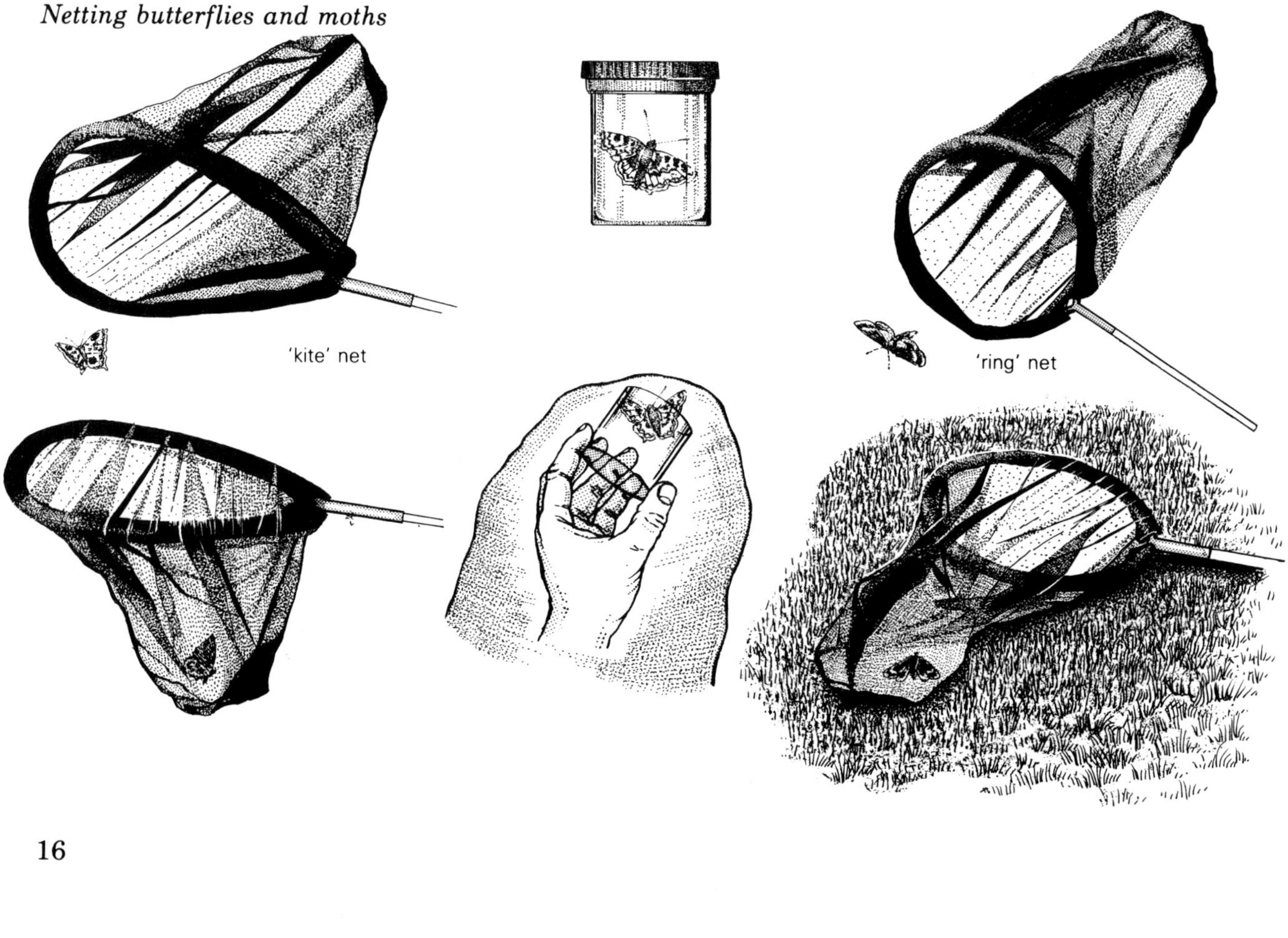

'kite' net

'ring' net

16

Once the butterfly is caught it can be transferred to a small pot for examination. Thrust the open pot into the body of the net whilst keeping the mouth almost closed. Once the insect is potted the lid can be put on. Even a small pot will contain enough air to sustain the insect while you examine it. Don't handle the insect or you may dislodge its fine wing scales. Always ensure that the pot is big enough to take the larger butterflies such as the Peacock. Once you have examined the specimen make sure that you release it in the area in which it was caught.

Night-flying moths are easier to catch than you might imagine. It is important to choose a suitable night for your first moth-catching attempt. The best results will be achieved if you choose a night in mid-summer when it is cloudy and warm and there is a slight breeze. 'Sugaring' is an exciting way of attracting moths. The sweet smelling 'sugar' is made by mixing black treacle and beer and adding rotting fruit. Experiment to see what sort of mixture you can make. The 'sugar' is then painted on to pieces of cardboard attached to fence posts or trees. Soon the moths will smell the mixture and come and feed. They can then be picked off the card, placed in pots and examined in torchlight.

Moths will also be attracted by a light. The easiest method is to leave your bedroom window open and a 100-watt lamp burning. A light will attract moths even in a busy town. If you want to catch moths in the countryside an oil lamp or a bright torch, placed in front of a white sheet will make a good moth lamp.

Moths will be difficult to identify to begin with but if you start in April or May when there are few species in flight you will gradually arrive at the correct identification and gain in confidence. Many moths can be identified from books – always check the month in which various moths fly. If you think you have found a Winter Moth in July you could be wrong! When you have identified your moths always be sure to release them in dense vegetation where they will not make an easy meal for the birds.

How to watch birds

Watching birds is very different from watching insects. Usually insects, even those that fly, can be watched quite easily and can be caught so that they can be looked at more carefully. Birds must *not* be caught so they have to be skilfully watched so that they are not scared and fly away.

You don't have to go out especially to watch birds as they can be seen when you are out of doors on the way to the shops or school or during your break times. Binoculars are not always needed, you can learn the general shapes and colours of birds without them.

If you want to watch birds very closely, though, you will need binoculars. Don't be in a hurry to buy a pair, watch without them for a while and then try out a variety of makes. The best way to do this is to make friends with local bird-watchers who will let you try theirs and will advise you. A pair of 8 x 30 mm binoculars will probably suit you. They are light, so that you can go out walking without being weighed down and they also allow you to look at birds that are near to you and those that are far away. If you buy a pair of binoculars test them first; be sure that the colours show up correctly when you look through the lenses.

It is very important to learn to use your binoculars correctly. Firstly the basic focusing of your binoculars must be set up. You will not have identical vision in both eyes so modern binoculars have both central focus adjustment and a screw focus on the right-hand lens. The focusing for each eye is done separately.

First make sure that the two eyepieces are in line with your eyes, now line your glasses up on an upright post or tree trunk some 15–20 m away. Cover the right-hand object lens (the large one at the front) with your right hand, and then look at the post, focusing with the centre wheel until you have a sharp image. Then cover the left-hand object lens with your left hand, look at the post and alter the screw on the right-hand eyepiece until you have a clear image.

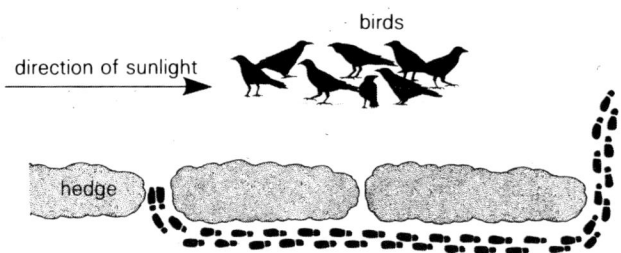

How to stalk birds

A good field guide, binoculars and a telescope are useful aids to bird study

Stalking birds

Make a note of the position of the right-hand eyepiece so that you can check that your binoculars are ready before going out to watch birds. Spectacle wearers should keep their glasses on when trying out binoculars and ask the sales assistant for advice.

Once you have your binoculars make sure that you keep the lenses clean with a soft cloth. You will soon get used to looking at birds through binoculars – practice makes perfect.

If you become very interested in watching sea-birds, ducks on reservoirs or waders on estuaries, you may decide to buy a telescope. Small, cheap telescopes with small lenses are a waste of money; wait until you can afford (or ask for) a larger instrument with an object lens which is at least 60 mm wide. You will probably need a tripod too. Don't forget that the sort of telescope star-watchers use is no good to the bird-watcher – the image is upsidedown!

There are two ways of watching birds at really close range; one is to go to bird-watching places that have 'hides', the other is to learn the art of stalking.

Many bird reserves have wooden hides from which you can watch in comfort. Remember not to open the flaps to the windows until the door is shut, so that it is as dark as possible in the hide. It is also important that you are quiet and that you keep your face and fingers well inside the hide. It is often possible, if you move slowly and quietly, to sit and watch birds from the edge of lakes, estuaries or in woodland clearings. Sitting quietly is often the best way to see birds – let them come to you!

If you are in open country, however, this is more difficult. This is where you need to stalk birds. Stalking is the art of seeing birds without them seeing you. Wear dull clothing, walk quietly and slowly and avoid stepping out into open spaces where you would show up against the background.

Try to approach birds with the sun on your back and the wind in your face. Birds are very difficult to identify as shapes against the sun, the colours do not show up and it is almost impossible to judge their size. If the wind is blowing towards you any noise you make is less likely to disturb the birds. Use the cover of the trees and bushes to approach the birds. When you come to open spaces, always look around first before you walk on, otherwise you may disturb nearby birds before you can have a good look at them. In thick vegetation like reed-beds, scrub and woodland don't go charging through the thickets but watch the edges where birds often feed.

Identifying birds

The plumage of a Fieldfare

Birds often fly off soon after you spot them so it is important to take a notebook out with you so that you can make a quick sketch and a note or two – don't rely on your memory. You will need to attempt to name birds when they are flying, sitting, swimming, feeding and sleeping. Sometimes the bird will be near, at other times far away. A very simple drawing – it does not have to be very 'special' – is often more helpful than a page of notes. Mark the main colours on your sketch and look for details like beak or foot shape.

Learn the names of the parts of a bird, this will help you describe the bird to other bird-watchers or help you when you read descriptions in bird books.

Try and make your notes in the same order every time.

1 What is the bird's shape?

   Is the bird thin or fat? Does it remind you of a bird you know?
   What is the size and shape of the beak?
   How long are the legs and neck?
   What shape is the wing?
   How long is the tail?
   What shape are its feet?

2 How big is the bird?

   Try and compare the bird with a nearby bird that you know well, perhaps a sparrow, pigeon or mallard.

3 Where are the coloured feathers?

   Try to draw a picture showing areas of white or brightly coloured feathers.

4 What other colours are there?

   Make a note of the colour of beak, legs and feet.

5 How does the bird behave?

   Does the bird walk, run or climb in a particular way?
   How does it feed?
   Does it fly in a particular way?

You won't *need* to make notes on every bird you see, some you will instantly recognize from pictures in books and others you will know already, even if you have only just begun bird-watching. I expect you already know the European Robin. It is a good idea to practise drawing and note-making on a bird you already know. You are sure to see some little detail you had not noticed before. Try looking for the grey feathers on a Robin – do you know where they are?

Identifying birds is not always easy. Young birds can be difficult to identify. They are often like the adult birds but their colours are duller. Some young birds, especially sea-birds, are very different from their parents. Adult Herring Gulls are pale grey and white but their young are brown. In some kinds of birds, such as the Chaffinch, the male and female are different – the male has bright colours but the female, which sits on the eggs, is duller. In species like this the young usually look like the female.

You will be able to get a lot of help from the many excellent bird books which are now on sale. Look for a 'field guide' which will give you a brief account of birds' habits as well as their appearance. Do not be too disappointed if you cannot identify all the birds you see. Some fly off very quickly or only show themselves a little at a time while skulking in the undergrowth. Sometimes it is impossible to see enough of the bird you are trying to identify – even very experienced bird-watchers are not able to name all the birds they see. It is best to be honest with yourself and only keep a permanent record of those birds that you are sure you have identified positively.

Try to write a description and draw a sketch of the finches shown here as though you are seeing them out of doors. Now compare your description with that in a bird book, you will soon improve. Try, too, to describe some of the common birds you see from the window. When you have written your description look at the birds' flight and feeding behaviour. Once your notebook has a few descriptions, and details of days out, write them in a permanent loose-leaf notebook or a hardback diary. In years to come you will enjoy reading through your old records.

21

Counting birds

Counting birds will be difficult at first but you will get better in time. When you are counting birds in your garden or street the numbers you find will only be the highest count for that particular moment. The birds of town and field are very active and the numbers change all the time. I once thought that five Great Tits fed in my garden but when a friend (a qualified bird-ringer) put up nets in the garden he caught twenty-seven!

Flocks of birds are easier to count than a scattered few. Try looking for Starlings returning to their roost in the evening. Count twenty-five or so birds and then see how many groups of twenty-five there are in the flock.

Visit a local pond or lake in the winter and try to count the number of ducks. Be careful though as the female ducks of many species are very similar at a distance. You may find that you have to count diving ducks (like the Pochard) a number of times as some of them may be underwater when you count. You will soon find that not only will your counting skills improve but so, too, will your powers of identification.

If you visit the sea-shore while you are on holiday try counting the sea-birds. Use your binoculars all the time as the birds may be a long way off. You will often find other bird-watchers at the coast – ask them to help you.

Try counting duck on a lake or stretch of open water

23

Migration

Migration (movement from one place to another) happens in spring and autumn when large numbers of birds fly great distances to a different part of the world. Many birds such as Swifts, Swallows and Martins make their nests and raise families in Britain and Europe during the summer months, when there are lots of insects to eat. In the autumn when insects are becoming hard to find the migrant birds fly off to Africa where there is plenty of food. In the spring they return to Europe to breed.

Look out for Swifts, Swallows and Martins in spring – make a note of the dates of the first arrivals and see if they match up with those on the maps below.

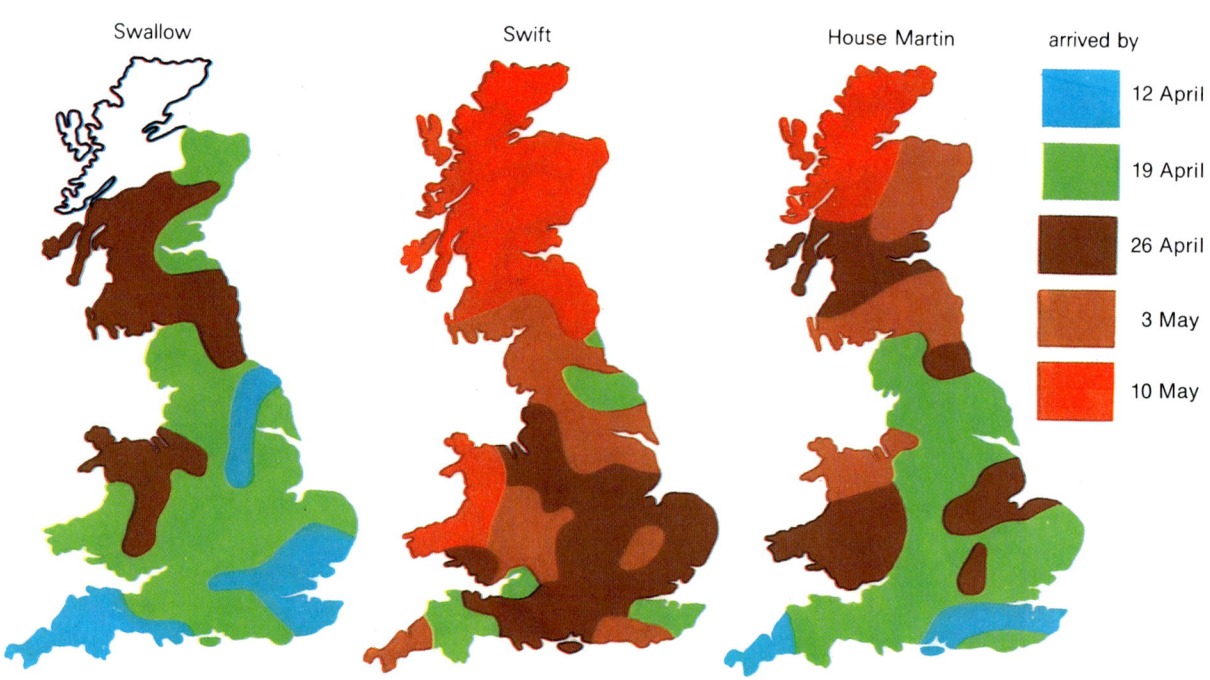

Dates of arrival of Swallow, Swift and House Martin

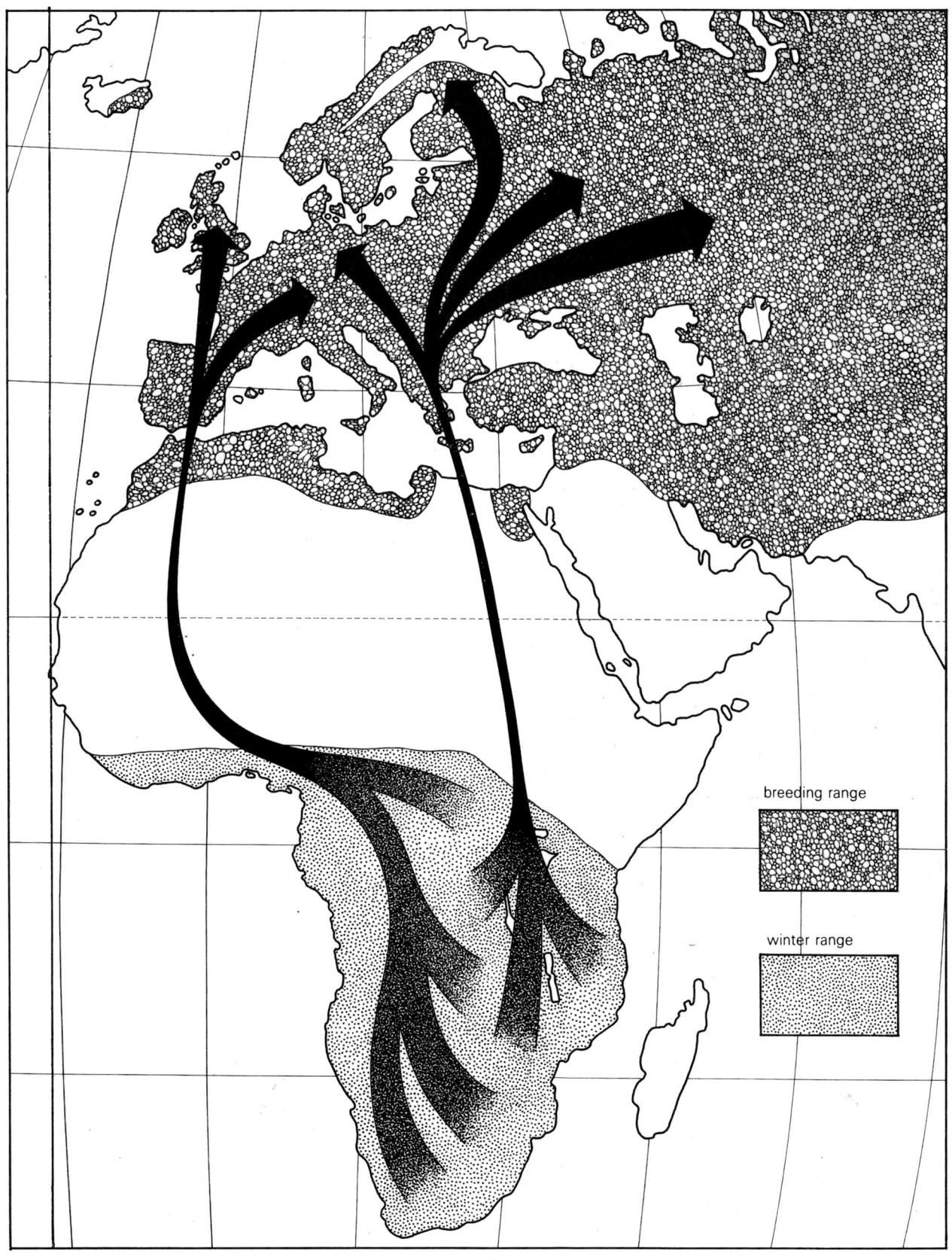

Spring migration of the Swallow

Feeding birds

House Sparrows feeding at the bird table

The best way to attract birds to your garden or yard is to feed them. Many birds die in the winter; the weather is cold, the days are short and food is scarce. Birds need to feed first thing in the morning as they use up a lot of energy at night just keeping warm.

Birds will eat a wide variety of food: nuts, seeds, scraps, and wild fruits collected from the countryside. The best time to collect food from the hedgerows is in the autumn, between about August and October. Look for the berries of Rowan (Mountain Ash), Blackthorn, Elderberry and Hawthorn and the nuts of Hazel, Beech, Oak, Horse and Sweet Chestnut. Crab apples and wild cherries are also full of goodness. The berries should be dried and stored in a dry, dark place.

Kitchen scraps are also good for birds – bones, meat and bacon are full of nourishment but they should be cooked first. Any form of fat will be greedily eaten by the birds. Cheese, oatmeal, bread, stale cake and cooked potatoes are also of value. Small birds, such as wintering Blackcaps, will even dig out the flesh from potato peelings. Peanuts, coconut and seeds of all sorts are attractive to Finches, Woodpeckers and the Tit family. Some foods, though, are harmful to birds, such as desiccated coconut, salted peanuts and large quantities of white bread.

You will attract more birds to your garden if you put the food in a number of places. Food hung on wires or placed in baskets will attract Tits, Woodpeckers and the more agile Finches like Greenfinch and Siskin. Food on bird-tables will attract a wide variety of species, including Crows, Thrushes, Finches and Sparrows. Birds like Pipits, Larks and Wagtails will readily feed on the ground. Only small quantities of food should be left on the ground, just enough to feed the birds for one day, otherwise rats may start to visit.

You should be careful where you place your bird-table; it should be where you can see it clearly, near enough to vegetation so that birds will feel safe when feeding but not so

A bird table adapted for a food-preference study

near that the local cats can hide while waiting to attack the birds.

A small, shallow water container should be placed on, or near the table as seed-eating birds need to drink regularly. While the birds drink or wash they will remain in view from the window for a little longer. Don't forget to break the ice if it freezes over.

Don't start feeding birds unless you are sure that you can accept the responsibility of providing food right through the winter (from about October to March). Once you attract birds to your garden you take them away from their usual feeding places and they come to rely on *you*. Don't feed birds in the summer when adult birds should be providing their young with rich animal food, such as worms and caterpillars.

You can soon discover which bird species are attracted to particular kinds of food. Divide your bird table into four sections by nailing battens on and then provide four types of food, perhaps bread, nuts, wheat and sunflower seed. You will be able to count the number of birds which eat each kind of food.

Once you have started feeding birds watch them carefully. Can you find out which species visit most often? Which food does each species prefer? Do some birds prefer to feed on hanging food, at the table or on the ground? Are some species more aggressive than others?

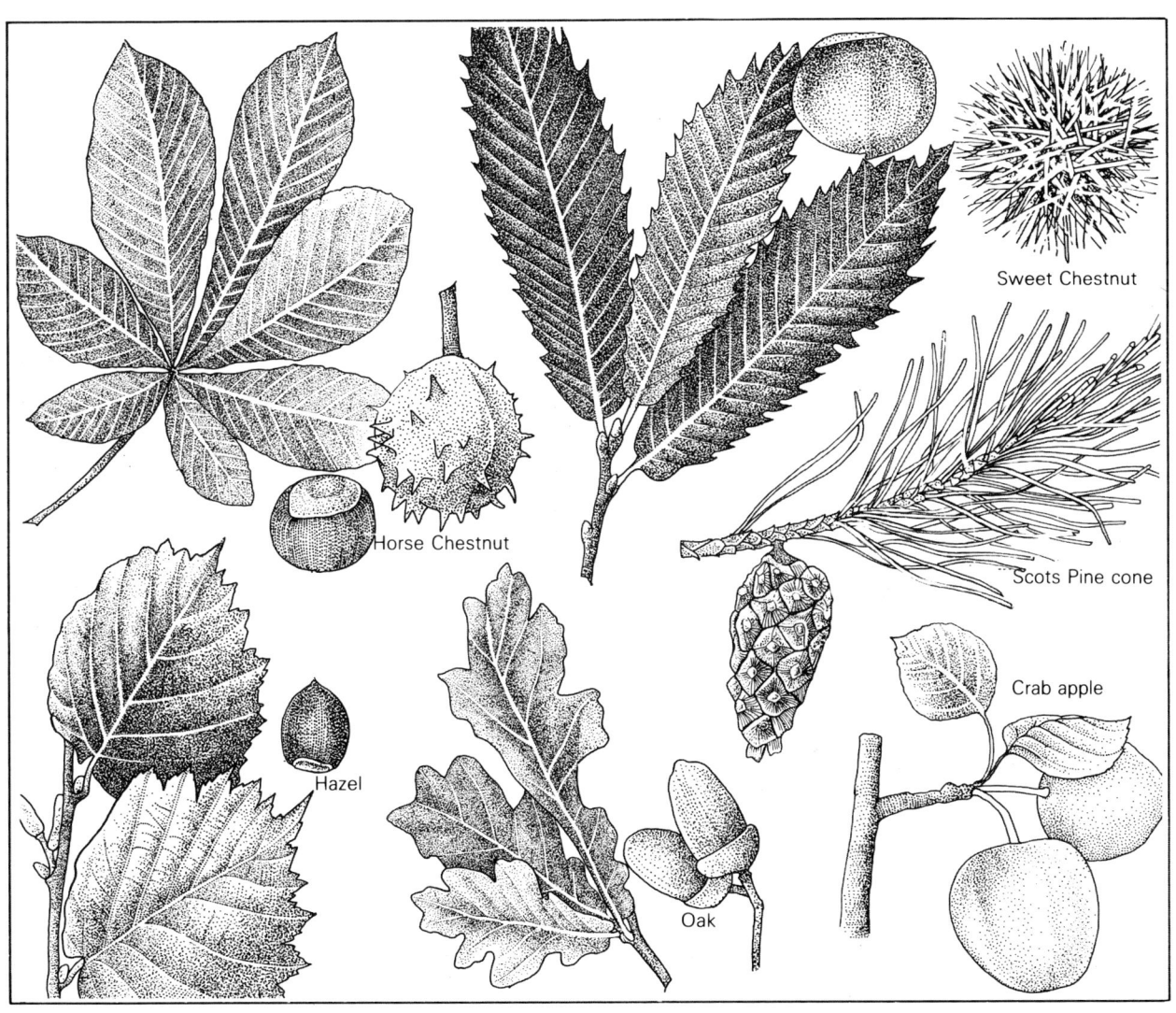

Birds breeding

Nests

In spring most birds prepare to breed, to produce a new generation of young birds. Usually the males decide on a breeding area – a territory. Inside this area the nest will be built and in many cases the adult birds will find food for the young from within its boundaries. The males cannot build a fence around their plot or post 'Keep Out' signs – however, they do manage to guard their area and find a mate, mainly by singing.

The male birds sing at various places on the edge of the territory, usually from obvious places like fence posts, chimney pots, bushes or the tops of reeds; these are called 'song posts'. They sing regularly to warn other males of the same species to keep away, and to find a mate. In the spring watch birds sing,

Male Reed Bunting singing

you will soon come to recognize the songs of the different species. You can even work out the area of a bird's territory by marking the 'song posts' on a sketch map and then joining them up. Birds defending their territory usually rely on song to keep other birds away but if this doesn't work they will display, waving their wings up and down, or spreading their tails to frighten visitors. If necessary they will even chase the offending bird out of the area.

When two birds have paired, they make a nest. It may be an open, cup-shape one like that of the Robin, a dome like that of the Long-tailed Tit, a hard mud container like that of the House Martin, or a hole as in the Kingfisher's nest. Usually the nest is lined with a soft material like moss, grass or feathers so that the eggs are well protected and warm. The female lays the eggs. One of the birds then sits on the eggs to keep them warm until they hatch. Sometimes the female sits on the eggs, sometimes the male and female take it in turns.

Once the eggs hatch the parents rear the young. The young of ducks, waders, gulls and game birds, like the pheasant, emerge from the egg with a covering of warm feathers, with their eyes open and able to run about; their parents soon encourage them to feed themselves. Song birds are born blind and naked – they have to be fed constantly by their doting parents.

Try to watch a pair of birds breeding. You don't need to disturb the nest, you can watch the parents defending their territory and carrying nesting material and food to the nest area. If you are lucky you will eventually see the young when they are ready to fly. Build yourself a nest box if you have space, this is sure to attract nesting birds – eventually.

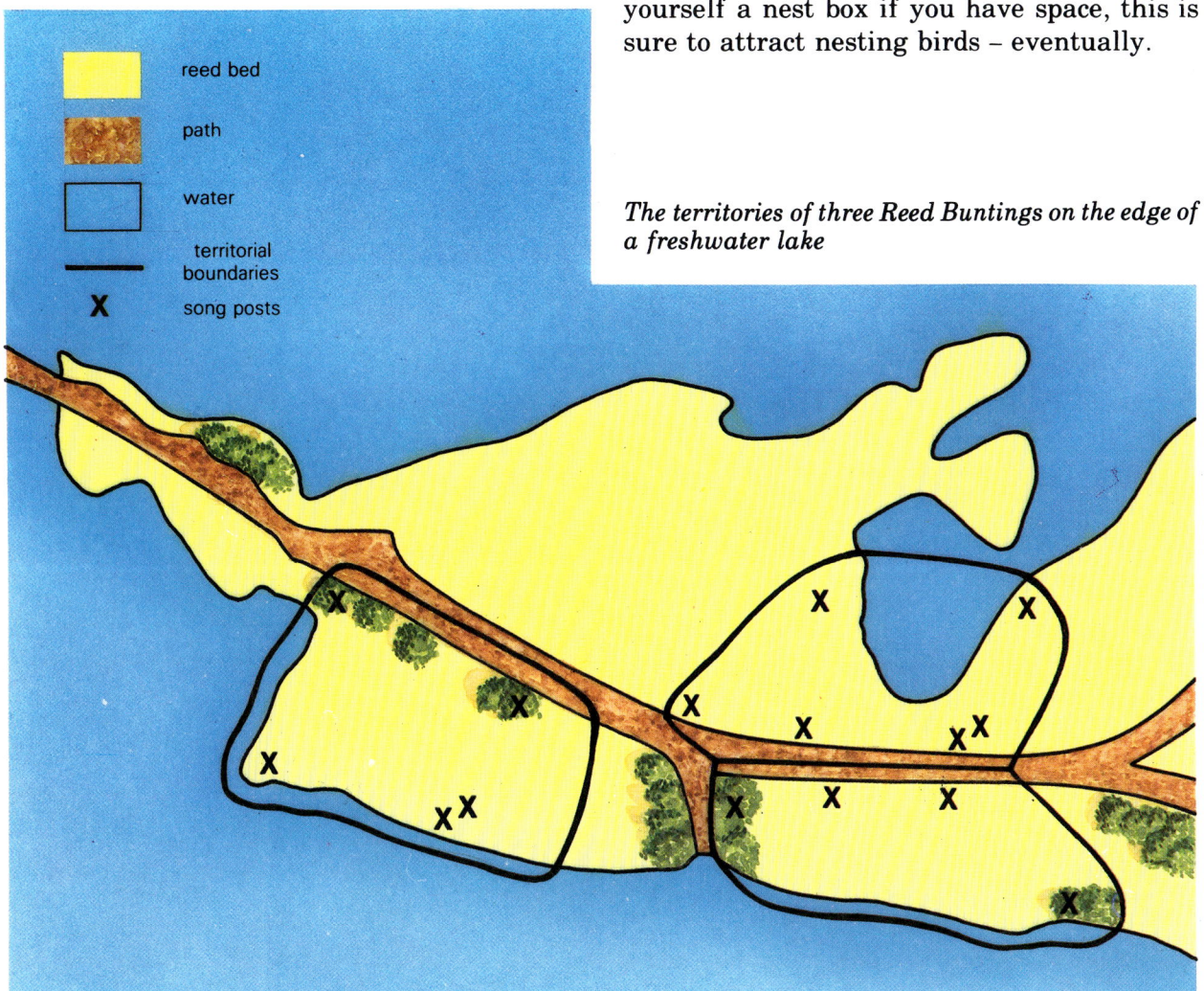

The territories of three Reed Buntings on the edge of a freshwater lake

Birds in flight

All animals are designed to fit into their place in nature. The wing and tail shape of birds vary according to the place in which they live and their life-style. Birds' beaks and feet also differ as birds eat a wide variety of foods in many types of landscape.

Most birds are designed to fly. They have light feathers, hollow bones, strong wing bones, massive chest muscles (the 'engines' of a bird) and extremely large lungs. The light structure of a bird is important because every gramme of weight a bird has to carry makes take-off more difficult. Feathers though are perhaps the key to a bird's flight. They are of three kinds: tough, flexible primary feathers which act as propellors; secondary feathers which cover the middle of the wing and keep the bird up in the air; and softer contour feathers which give the bird its streamline appearance and prevent its body heat from escaping. The strong tail feathers also act as a rudder and as air brakes.

Most woodland birds, like the Wren, have short, square-ended wings which give them the agility to fly through areas of thick vegetation.

Game birds, like the Pheasant, which spend much of their life on the ground (and make a good meal for a fox) also have short, broad wings which give them a very fast take-off when alarmed.

Birds, such as Swifts, which catch flying insects have long, pointed wings which, as their name suggests, gives them great speed in the air.

Herons, which catch large fish, have broad wings so that they can carry the heavy load back to the young. The large area of Herons' wings causes them to fly with slow, deep, wing-beats.

Sea-birds have a variety of wing shapes. The long, thin wings of the Fulmar enable it to glide over the sea for hours on end. Only in very light winds does it need to flap its wings regularly. The Razorbill, on the other hand, has wings with which it swims underwater, chasing fish. These wings are strong and short. This is an ideal shape for a swimming limb but less well designed for flight. The Razorbill, therefore, has to flap its wings very fast in order to fly over the waves.

Birds of prey also vary. Eagles and Buzzards have broad wings which help them soar high over hills searching for their prey. Hawks, like the Sparrow Hawk, also have broad wings with rounded tips so that they are very skilful at flying through the woodlands in which they hunt. Falcons, such as the Peregrine Falcon have long pointed wings so that they can dive at great speeds on other flying birds. The Kestrel, which is also a falcon, has long pointed wings and a long, broad tail so that it can hover while searching for small mice and voles in grassland.

Migrant birds tend to have longer wings than 'stay-at-home' types. The Swallows and

Birds in flight

Martins that hunt for flying insects, have long, thin, pointed wings, not only to give them the speed to catch insects but to enable them to cross the desert areas of North Africa as quickly as possible. The Hobby (a falcon) is also a migrant and it too has long, thin, pointed wings which allow it to fly so fast that it can catch Swallows, Martins and large flying insects such as Dragonflies. It, too, moves quickly between Europe and southern Africa.

When you are out watching birds look at the wing shapes and the style of flight of a wide range of birds. See if you can find a link between these features. Finches and Woodpeckers are heavy birds with fairly small wings – how does that show up in their flight? Flight is not only a means of getting from place to place – watch the Skylark singing in flight and the Spotted Flycatcher swooping out from a branch to catch insects.

Birds' beaks

If all birds looked alike they would all be eating the same food; there would not be enough to go around and many would starve. In fact birds have become adapted in many ways to take advantage of all the different types of food and habitats. Different groups of birds have different shaped beaks. Many species have such specialized beaks that they can only feed on one type of food, others have beaks with which they can eat almost anything.

The Blackbird has a 'general purpose' beak. It is of medium-length and sharp, ideal for picking up seeds, berries and insects or for tearing at leaves. Most of the other field and woodland birds have more specialized beaks. Finches have beaks like a pair of pliers with which they can crack open seeds. There is a lot of variety, however, within this family. The Goldfinch has a fine pointed beak which it uses to extract the very small seeds of thistles from the dry flower head. The Crossbill, a bird of pine forests, has crossed mandibles (the upper and lower parts of the beak) so that it can tear open ripe cones and pull out the seeds. The Hawfinch has a beak like a vice so that it can crack open the hardest seeds, it even cracks cherry stones! Many woodland birds, like Warblers and the Goldcrest have fine tweezer-like bills that they use for catching very small insects. The Nuthatch and Woodpeckers also eat insects but they have beaks like chisels with which they hammer holes in rotting wood so that they can pull out the worm-like larvae of wood-boring beetles. Many species catch insects in flight. The Swift has a very wide mouth so that when it is flying rapidly it 'trawls' up hundreds of small insects and then rolls them into a ball with its tongue so that it can return to its nest and feed its young.

Wading birds feed mainly on small animals in mud, in water, or on the surface of sandy or

stony shores. The Plovers have short, sharp beaks for picking up food from the surface, but birds like the Woodcock have longer beaks so that they can dig for worms. The Avocet also has a long beak but it does not dig for food but sweeps its beak from side to side sieving small animals from the shallow lagoons in which it lives.

Ducks and geese feed in a variety of ways. Most ducks feed on water plants and seeds. The Shoveller is very well adapted for eating floating seeds and small animals; it swims along with its beak on the water surface filtering out food through sieves on the edge of its wide, flat bill. Geese actually cut up water plants or grass with their scissor-like beaks. Some ducks, such as the Red-breasted Merganser, actually catch fish so they have long, thin beaks lined with horny spikes which stop the fish from escaping.

Many other birds eat fish. The two best-known inland fishermen are the Kingfisher and the Heron, both have long pointed beaks, just like daggers. Out at sea fish are caught by birds which 'fly' underwater chasing their prey. One of these is the Puffin, which has a short beak like a clamp so that once a fish is caught it cannot escape. Gannets dive from the air to catch fish with their spear-like beaks.

Birds of prey, like the Buzzard have sharp, curved beaks to tear up the flesh of their victims.

Beaks are also used during nest-building. Most birds weave twigs, grass, moss and other similar materials into a cup-shaped nest. Many, though, build totally different structures. The Woodpeckers, most of the Tit family, the Kingfisher and Sand Martin nest in holes – usually dug out with their beaks. The Long-tailed Tit builds a dome-shaped nest with moss, hair, feathers and lichens all held together with spiders' webs. House Martins and Nuthatches even use mud in the building of their nests.

Birds' feet

The shape of birds' feet varies according to the places in which they live and their life-style. They are used to move from place to place, to walk, swim, wade and climb. They are also used in nest-building, feeding and preening – looking after their feathers.

More than half of the world's bird species are in the passerine group – the perching birds. The Robin has three forward facing toes and one that faces backwards. This enables the bird to walk, hop, climb and hold on to a branch – to perch. It even has a locking mechanism which allows it to sleep while perching.

Many species have more specialized feet. The Treecreeper has very sharp claws on toes which can be flattened against upright surfaces; this enables it to climb up trees and walls in search of insects. Woodpeckers have two forward-facing and two backward-facing toes so that they can grip the bark of trees very firmly. Woodpeckers and the Treecreeper both have very stiff tails that they use as a third leg when climbing.

Swifts spend almost all their lives in flight and only land to build a nest, lay eggs and rear their young. The nest is built in a hole in a building or on a cliff face. The feet of the Swift are short and held close to the body. The toes are very short but tipped with extremely sharp claws, consequently they can only hang on upright surfaces. In order to take off they launch themselves from vertical walls and cliffs. If you ever find one which has landed on the ground pick it up and launch it into the air or it will surely die.

Birds of prey like the Golden Eagle have strong toes with sharp claws known as talons. When they swoop on hares or grouse they grip them with their powerful talons until the life is crushed out of them. The fish-eating Osprey

34

has sharp spines on the pads of its feet to prevent its slippery prey from escaping.

Many birds live in or near water and therefore need quite different feet from the perching birds.

Waders spend most of their life walking or standing on the soft mud of estuaries or in ploughed fields and marshland. The Curlew has three long, forward-pointing toes and a very short hind toe. As the front toes spread out they prevent the bird from sinking into the mud. The Avocet which feeds in deeper water and often swims has similar feet but there are small webs between the toes.

The Coot lives in deep water and on the water's edge. It has lobes of leathery skin on each of its toes so that it can spread its weight out when walking on mud and also swim and dive in search of food. The Great-crested Grebe spends nearly all its life in the water and has, therefore, larger lobes on its toes. Its feet are set well back on its body which enables it to paddle strongly but makes it rather clumsy on land. The Mallard is a powerful swimmer, having large webs between its front three toes. The Cormorant, which dives beneath the surface of the sea in search of fish, has all four toes facing forward, all of which have webs.

Birds use their beaks and claws to comb their feathers into good order. This is known as preening. Herons and Nightjars have a 'comb' on one of their claws which helps them to preen very efficiently.

Birds' feet and beaks are very difficult to see in the wild but can easily be seen in museum collections. Most museums now arrange their birds in displays showing the habitats in which they live so you will be able to see the bird in its proper setting. You can get an excellent view of birds' feet and beaks in action if you visit a zoo or bird reserve.

Mammals in the garden

Most British mammals are small and very active but they often feed at night or in thick vegetation. At first you will not see them but they are there in larger numbers than you could believe possible. All gardens are homes to mammals, even those in the centre of town. Mammals have regular habits so even though they are seldom seen they leave signs of their presence. Mammals can be encouraged to live in any garden if they are provided with food and shelter.

Badgers are fairly common in town gardens. They are noted for the regularity with which they use pathways. Look out for these paths, and if you find one, put a badger-gate in the fence so that the animal can use its usual route with ease.

Food-bearing trees such as Beech and Hazel will also attract mammals. You will also find that 'pests' like snails, slugs and leather jackets (cranefly grubs) will be eaten by the

Mammals will live in a garden if access, food and shelter are provided

Many town gardens will attract foxes, badgers and hedgehogs

smaller mammals. Shelter is also important; small mammals, such as voles and wood mice, will flourish if small areas of uncut grass and piles of hedge cuttings are left in garden corners. The earths of foxes are often to be found under garden sheds.

Badgers, foxes and hedgehogs will eat scraps. The food should be placed quite close to vegetation and near a window so that you can watch the animals feeding. Hedgehogs are attracted to a shallow dish containing bread and milk.

It is also important to provide drinking water for mammals. An old dustbin lid set into the lawn will provide a suitable drinking place, as will a garden pond if one edge is allowed to slope gently into the water.

Make sure you do not provide too much food or you will attract rats. Though rats are as interesting to watch as other mammals they tend to carry diseases and, therefore, should not be encouraged to live close to your home.

Foxes and badgers, together with domestic cats and dogs, can also be a nuisance as they will raid dustbins unless the tops are secure.

Many gardens with mature trees play host to Grey Squirrels. They store seeds and berries for the winter and scurry through the tree-tops in the autumn. They will eat buds but do little harm unless short of food in the winter when they will strip the bark from young trees. If you have nest boxes in your garden they may need metal plates around the holes to prevent squirrels gnawing their way to the young birds.

Mammals are probably more easily watched in gardens than in any other location as they remain wild yet get used to people, noise and electric lights.

Small mammals

British scientists call shrews, mice and voles 'small mammals'. Watching these mammals is difficult but rewarding.

Shrews are small and dark, have small heads and pointed snouts. They are 'insectivores', insect-eaters, although this is rather a misleading name as in addition to insects they eat worms and many other invertebrates. They have sharp, pointed teeth to crunch up their prey.

Mice and voles are rodents. They have flat teeth with deep grooves to enable them to gnaw hard plant stems and leaves. Mice have large ears and eyes, pointed snouts and long tails. Voles have more pointed snouts, smaller eyes and pointed ears.

Most small mammals live in rough grass areas, often making their nests at the end of long, hidden runs. Voles are particularly fond of passages in long grass. If you find one don't walk on it, you will destroy the signs left by

A Field Vole at large

the animal. Walk very slowly alongside it in a parallel line. If you find a grass nest don't touch it as you may leave your scent on the grass and scare off the owner. Watch and listen and you may hear young voles calling. Always look in small holes at the base of trees or in banks, they may reveal small mammals. The House Mouse will be found in sheds, outbuildings and anywhere where grain is stored.

Voles leave many signs of their presence. Field Voles eat summer grass but in winter they eat bark, rushes, the woody stems of raspberry canes and even the occasional invertebrate. In summer the presence of Field Voles is indicated by piles of olive green droppings covered with chopped grass.

Bank Voles eat Hazel nuts, gnawing the tops of the shell, leaving teeth marks on the inside of the hole. The Wood Mouse gnaws the side of the nut, leaving teeth marks on the outside of the hole.

Look out for Water Voles in streams or river-sides. They are about the size of a rat but they have shaggy fur, short ears and a shorter tail than a rat. They are expert swimmers.

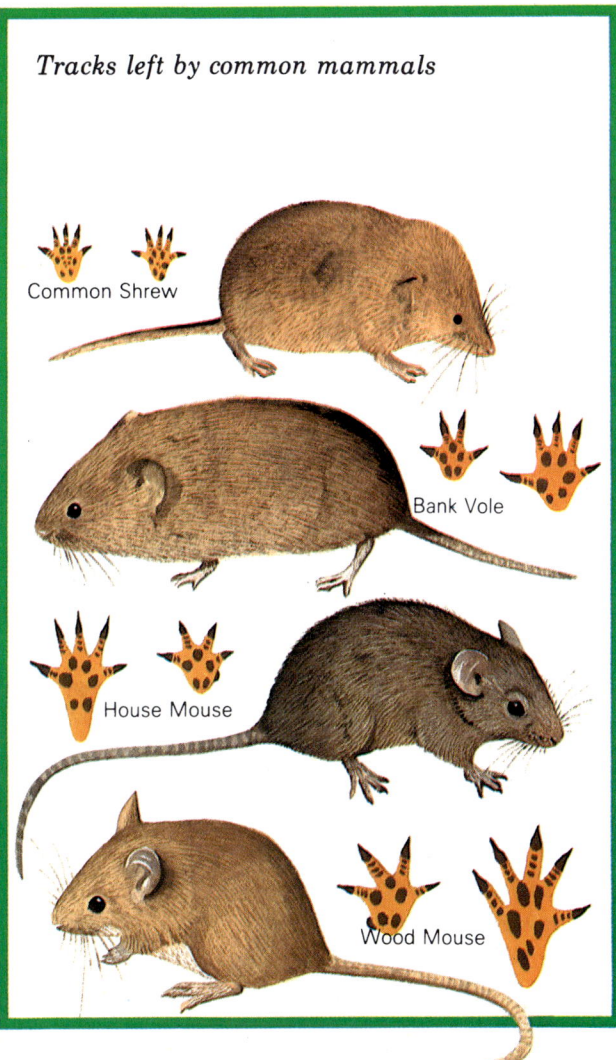

Tracks left by common mammals

Common Shrew

Bank Vole

House Mouse

Wood Mouse

Collecting evidence

As mammals are so secretive, or active only at night, much of our knowledge of them comes from the signs that they leave behind.

The most easily read signs are footprints. When you find a set of tracks take care not to tread on any of the prints. Make a careful sketch and measure the distance between individual tracks. This will enable you not only to identify the owner of the track but the manner in which it was moving. Some animals drag their tails, leaving a trail – make sure you include this in your sketch.

A permanent record of a track can be made by making a plaster cast. Find a clear print

A plaster cast of a badger's footprint

Tracks and prints of some familiar mammals

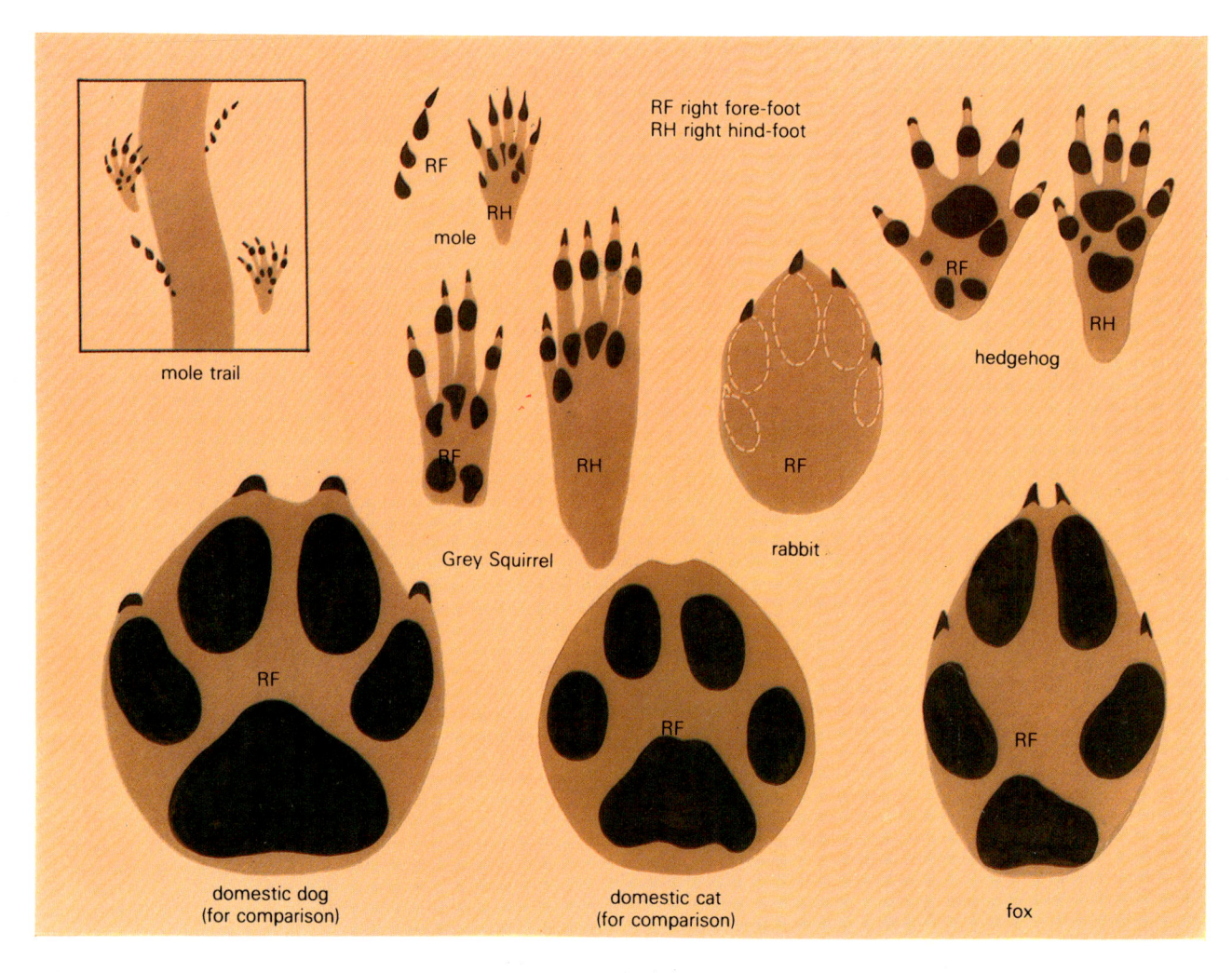

RF right fore-foot
RH right hind-foot

mole trail

mole

Grey Squirrel

rabbit

hedgehog

domestic dog
(for comparison)

domestic cat
(for comparison)

fox

40

A small mammal caught in a bottle

and remove any pieces of grass or twigs from the impression. Then 'fence' round the print with a circle of card fastened with a paper clip. If the ground is soft press the card into the earth, if it is hard pile some earth around the outside of the card circle to make a seal. Now mix up some plaster of Paris or dental plaster if you can find it. Put a little water into a bowl and add the plaster until it forms an island in the middle, then mix the two together until creamy. Now fill the card mould to the top, making sure that you remove the air bubbles by gently tapping the top of the card circle. At first the plaster will be warm, when it is cold it will have set and can be removed and wrapped in paper. Don't be in too much of a hurry to see the results, leave it for several hours until it is really hard. Any soil that has stuck to the plaster can be removed with an old, damp toothbrush.

The remains of small mammals can be very informative. Look out for abandoned bottles, they often contain the skeletons of mice and shrews which have become trapped. The bones of mice and voles can also be found in owl pellets. Owls **regurgitate** (bring back up from the stomach) the fur and bones they cannot digest as a pellet. These will be found near owls' nests. The easiest way to identify the contents of pellets and bottles is to place the remains in a dish with a little disinfectant and look for the skulls. These can be identified with the help of a book. The bones make a nice display if bleached with a weak solution of kitchen bleach, rinsed and left to dry and then glued to a piece of black card.

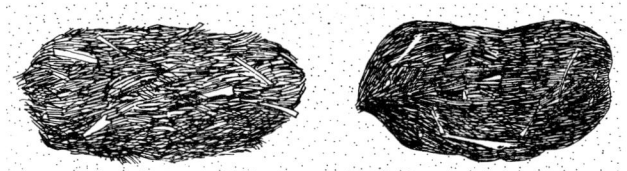

Owl pellets

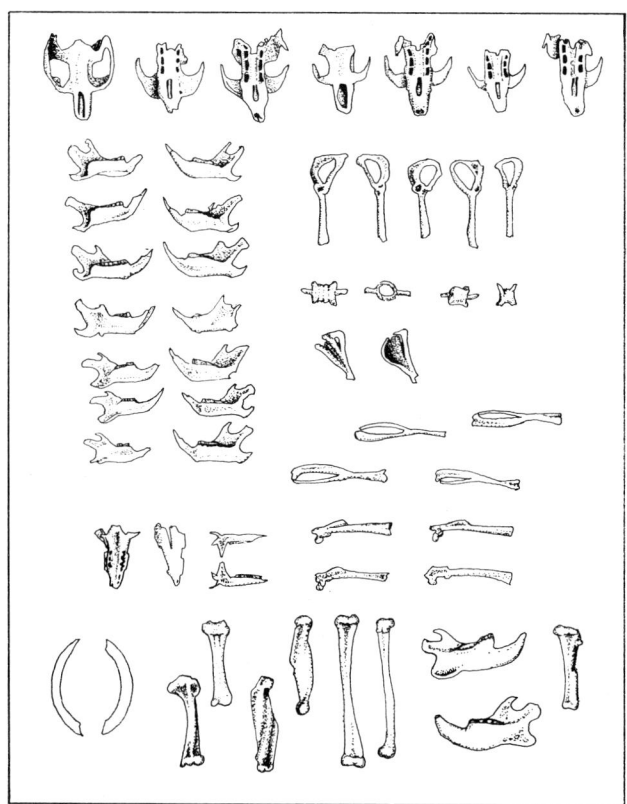

The contents of an owl pellet

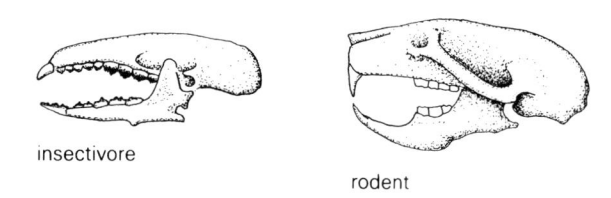

insectivore

rodent

Identifying small mammals

41

Watching mammals

Mammal watching is probably the most difficult of the naturalists' skills to master. Most mammals have good eyesight and hearing and a very acute sense of smell; they are, therefore, difficult to approach.

The best way to start watching mammals is to get used to observing the tamer species. The Grey Squirrel is usually easy to watch in summer. Look in town parks and in small woods on the edge of towns. Sit still on the edge of a woodland clearing or next to the bigger parkland trees and you will almost certainly see squirrels chasing through the branches or searching for food in the leaf litter beneath the trees. Look out for large bundles of twigs, the drey, in which the young squirrels spend their infancy.

Many country parks hold herds of deer. Red and Fallow Deer are often seen in large numbers in lowland estates and Roe and Sika Deer can be seen in smaller groups if you are lucky. Watching wild deer is more difficult, except in places like the New Forest where they have become accustomed to tourists and people generally.

Rabbits and hares are usually easy to watch from cars, especially early in the morning. The edges of sandy golf courses often provide the right conditions for rabbits, but look out for flying golf balls and don't trespass. If you are prepared to sit quietly it is possible to watch Bank Voles feeding in the daytime. Look for their signs in sheltered, shaded areas with a covering of long grass and shrubs. When walking along rivers or canals be on the watch for the larger Water Vole.

Foxes and Badgers are most active at dawn and dusk. If you want to watch them then you will need to be well prepared. Dark, warm clothing is essential. An anorak with a hood is ideal as once the hood is raised the outline of the head is obscured. Warm trousers, gloves and a scarf are also vital as, even in the summer, it can be very cold in the early or late hours of the day. If you are aiming to watch Badgers at dusk, wait until early spring, find out where their setts are from local naturalists and then visit the area in the daytime. Select a number of comfortable hiding places and remove any fallen twigs from the approaches. Good preparations are very important.

Before going out in the evening have a warm drink and be sure that Mum or Dad know what they're letting themselves in for when they come with you!

Aim to be at the site about an hour before dusk. Once you have arrived walk carefully, avoid talking and don't let anyone smoke.

A Bank Vole

A Wood Mouse feeding at night

Badger-watching at dusk

Select one of your watching places. Be sure that the wind is blowing towards you so that your scent and any sound you make will be blown away. With luck you will soon see the Badgers emerging for their evening's hunting. Once they have gone, see if you can attract Wood Mice. Put down a piece of card with a pile of seeds on it and wait for a movement. If a mouse does come it can be watched by torchlight.

Bats are easily watched but very difficult to identify. They are best seen at dusk and can be found in towns, wooded areas and especially over ponds and lakes. Bats have a form of echo-location which allows them to hunt and navigate in the dark. The signals they send out cannot be heard by humans as they are too high. Listen out for bat calls though, these are high-pitched but within our hearing range, especially while we are young.

If you see a bat in your garden put up a bat box. Bat boxes are similar to bird boxes, but they have a slit at the bottom and a roughened vertical landing stage. The bats spend the day clinging to the rough back with the sharp claws of their feet. If you watch the boxes in the late evening you should see the bats fly out to hunt. Under no circumstances should you disturb the bats while they are in the boxes.

Animals living together – an Oak tree

As you spend more time looking at wildlife you will probably find that you enjoy watching particular animals – butterflies and birds are very popular. It is very important, though, to remember that all living things depend on each other and on their surroundings. The soil supports plants, which are eaten by herbivores which are preyed upon by carnivores. When the plants and animals die they decompose and enrich the soil; nothing is wasted.

Even a single Oak is a community. Many shade-loving plants, fungi, ferns and lichens find a home on, or beneath, the tree.

Insects abound. The Oak Leaf Roller larvae roll up Oak leaves and live within them, eating their way through their shelter. The larva of the common Footman moth feeds on the dry lichens growing on the tree's trunk and branches. The Gall wasp lays its eggs in the Oak buds and an Oak marble gall is produced as a home for the developing larva. The Cockchafer grubs eat the tree's roots and the adults its leaves.

Squirrels eat acorns, leaves and young birds, while beneath the tree Wood Mice eat seeds, fruit and invertebrates and are pursued by the Weasel.

In and around the Oak the tits search for small insects, the Woodpeckers probe the bark and search for grubs and the Jay carries acorns to its winter store. High up in the canopy the noisy young Crows await their food-bearing parents.

The Oak is the finest of all European trees. It plays host to more species of flowering plants, lichens, fungi and ferns than any other species. As a result it is a community in itself, visited by vast numbers of invertebrate species, especially insects and the birds and mammals which feed on them. If you have a large garden and you want to attract wildlife try planting an Oak tree – remember, though, that it may eventually grow to twenty-one metres in height.

Carrion Crow
Red Squirrel
Great Spotted Woodpecker
Poor Man's Beefsteak
Common Footman
Oak Leaf Roller
Oak Marble Gall
Enchanter's Nightshade
Weasel
Wood Mouse
C.J.S.

Animals living together – a downland

The best way to watch animals is to find a small area close to your home and spend as much time there as possible. This is far better than rushing around the countryside. Get to know your own 'patch' well so that visits to other habitats will then be much more instructive. Not only will you have practised the techniques of watching but you will have an area to use as a comparison with new sites.

In every habitat animals and plants live as a well-balanced community – an ecosystem. On a chalk downland the soil is chalky, the landscape is open and dry and therefore only certain species of plants and animals can thrive there. The thin chalk soil is ideal for grasses and low shrubs. Within the grasses grow Wild Thyme, Thistles, Orchids, Birdsfoot Trefoil and a host of other low-growing flowers. These plants attract a wide variety of insects. The elegant Chalkhill Blue butterfly lays its eggs on the colourful low-lying Birdsfoot Trefoil and the pale green caterpillars eat the foliage. The Skippers live on grasses.

Sheep, rabbits and Short-tailed Voles graze the grasslands. Where these grazers are scarce, though, the grass grows longer and shrubs begin to grow. Bramble, Gorse, Hawthorn and wild roses establish themselves and give shelter to Yellowhammers and Whitethroats. The Yellowhammer, a member of the bunting family, feeds mainly on seed but also eats invertebrates, mainly insects. The Whitethroat is a warbler which eats a wide variety of invertebrates. In the open grassland the Skylark can be found rising quickly into the air and singing loudly as it floats to the ground.

Hiding in the bushes or soaring high overhead are the predators. The Fox skulks in the undergrowth seeking voles and rabbits, the Kestrel hovers over unsuspecting mice, voles and occasionally small birds. High overhead the Buzzard patrols its territory looking for rabbits.

The plants – the foundation for every ecosystem – use sunlight and chemicals to produce sugar in their leaves and are known as 'producers'. The animals that eat plants (the herbivores), and the animals that eat other animals (carnivores), are all known as 'consumers'. Plants and animals in an ecosystem depend on each other.

Ecosystems change as time passes, they never stand still. Each habitat goes through a process known as succession. For example, in most of England the natural landscape was Oak woodland. This would be the case today if humans had not altered the shape of the countryside. Farming, house building and industry has changed the 'face' of England.

Look at your 'patch' and see if you can spot change at work. If it is an open field which is not being grazed watch how the Sycamore and Ash seedlings start to spread.

You will by this time be confident enough to identify a variety of animals and some wild plants. Now try and make links between

A downland ecosytem

plants and animals. Look at your local Stinging Nettle beds and try to discover which butterfly caterpillars are eating the leaves. What do Ladybirds eat when they appear on the rose bushes in your garden or the local park? Watch the Rowan trees in the autumn and try and identify all the birds which come to eat the bright red berries.

Try and make the most of your natural surroundings whether it is open, rolling fields and the soaring Skylark or Buddleia struggling to grow in a brick wall and strutting town pigeons. Remember, tomorrow is *your* future.

Suggested further reading

Insects
Butterflies and Moths, J. Leigh Pemberton (Ladybird, 1979)
Insects – Clue Book, Gwen Allen & Joan Denslow (Oxford University Press, 1969)
Insect Watching – Nature Trail Book, Ruth Thomson (Usborne, 1976)
The Oxford Book of Insects, John Burton (Oxford University Press, 1973)

Birds
Birds and How They Live, F. E. Newing & R. Bowood (Ladybird, 1966)
Bird – Clue Book, Gwen Allen & Joan Denslow (Oxford University Press, 1968)
Birdwatching – Nature Trail Book, Malcom Hart (Usborne, 1976)
The Birdlife of Britain, P. Hayman & P. Burton (Mitchell Beazley, 1976)

Mammals
Collins' Guide to Animal Tracks and Signs, P. Bang & P. Dahlstrom (Collins, 1974)
Tracks and Signs – Clue Book, Gwen Allen & Joan Denslow (Oxford University Press, 1975)

Ecology
Nature's Roundabout – an introduction to Ecology, Patrick Armstrong (Ladybird, 1979)
The Young Ecologist, Neil Arnold (Ward Lock Ltd, 1981)
Nature at Work – an introduction to Ecology, British Museum (Cambridge University Press, 1978)
The Family Naturalist, Michael Chinery (Macdonald & Jane's, 1977)

Useful addresses

Watch
22 The Green, Nettleham, Lincoln LN2 2NR
Organizes environmental projects for young people.

Wildfowl Trust
Slimbridge, Gloucestershire
The Trust has very good educational facilities in a number of centres throughout Britain.

Young Ornithologists' Club
(YOC) The Lodge, Sandy, Bedfordshire
The junior branch of the Royal Society for the Protection of Birds (RSPB). One of the largest and best junior wildlife organizations in the world.